I SPOT SHAPES!

I SPOT CIRCLES

first concepts

BY NATALIE HUMPHREY

Gareth Stevens
PUBLISHING

Circles are everywhere!
The frisbee is a circle.

The coin is a circle.

4

The wheel is a circle.

7

The cookie is a circle.

9

The hoop is a circle.

The donut is a circle.

13

The mirror is a circle.

15

The button is a circle.

17

The waffle is a circle.

19

The pizza is a circle.

21

Can you spot
the circles?

23

Please visit our website, www.garethstevens.com. For a free color catalog of all our high-quality books, call toll free 1-800-542-2595 or fax 1-877-542-2596.

Library of Congress Cataloging-in-Publication Data
Names: Humphrey, Natalie, author.
Title: I spot circles / Natalie Humphrey.
Description: Buffalo, New York : Gareth Stevens Publishing, [2025] | Series: I spot shapes | Includes index.
Identifiers: LCCN 2023044271 (print) | LCCN 2023044272 (ebook) | ISBN 9781538291689 (library binding) | ISBN 9781538291672 (paperback) | ISBN 9781538291696 (ebook)
Subjects: LCSH: Circle–Juvenile literature. | Shapes–Juvenile literature.
Classification: LCC QA484 .H86 2025 (print) | LCC QA484 (ebook) | DDC 516/.154–dc23/eng/20231031
LC record available at https://lccn.loc.gov/2023044271 LC ebook record available at https://lccn.loc.gov/2023044272

Published in 2025 by
Gareth Stevens Publishing
2544 Clinton Street
West Seneca, NY 14224

Designer: Leslie Taylor
Editor: Natalie Humphrey

Photo credits: Cover taka1022/Shutterstock.com; p. 3 wavebreakmedia/Shutterstock.com; p. 5 Vika-Viktoria/Shutterstock.com; p. 7 Africa Studio/Shutterstock.com; p. 9 VGstockstudio/Shutterstock.com; p. 11 alexei_tm/Shutterstock.com; p. 13 VasiliyBudarin/Shutterstock.com; p. 15 LediLena/Shutterstock.com; p. 17 Fernando Astasio Avila/Shutterstock.com; p. 19 Leanne8/Shutterstock.com; p. 21 grey_and/Shutterstock.com; p. 23 ilona.shorokhova/Shutterstock.com.

Printed in the United States of America

CPSIA compliance information: Batch #CSGS25: For further information contact Gareth Stevens, New York, New York at 1-800-542-2595.

Find us on